THE TOAST OF THE KIT-CAT CLUB

Linda France was born in 1958 in Newcastle. After living in Dorset, Leeds, London and Amsterdam, she returned to the North East in 1981, and has been based in Northumberland ever since. She currently lives in a cottage overlooking the Tyne Valley, a short walk from Hadrian's Wall.

She won the Basil Bunting Award in 1988 and 1989 and was awarded a Northern Arts Fellowship at the Tyrone Guthrie Centre in Ireland in 1990. She received the Arts Foundation's first Poetry Fellowship in 1993. She has worked on many collaborations with visual artists, particularly Birtley Aris on *Acknowledged Land*, *Storyville* and *wild* (Sand Press, 2004). She has a special interest in Poetry in Public Spaces, has been involved in over 20 different projects and teaches on the subject at the University of Newcastle upon Tyne.

Bloodaxe Books have published her anthology *Sixty Women Poets* (1993), a Poetry Book Society Special Commendation, as well as five other poetry books: her first collection, *Red* (1992); *The Gentleness of the Very Tall* (1994), a Poetry Book Society Recommendation; *Storyville* (1997); *The Simultaneous Dress* (2002); and *The Toast of the Kit-Cat Club* (2005). Her Indian pamphlet, *Aerogramme*, was published by Talking Pen in 2004.

She writes a regular feature on the craft of poetry for *Mslexia* magazine. In 1996 she wrote *Diamonds in Your Pockets* for Théâtre sans Frontières and *I am Frida Kahlo* for Cloud 9 Theatre Company in 2002. She is currently working on her first novel.

LINDA FRANCE

THE Toast OF THE Kit-Cat Club

A LIFE OF LADY MARY WORTLEY MONTAGU
IN ELEVEN CHAPTERS

BLOODAXE BOOKS

ISBN: 1 85224 677 4

First published 2005 by
Bloodaxe Books Ltd,
Highgreen,
Tarset,
Northumberland NE48 1RP.

www.bloodaxebooks.com
For further information about Bloodaxe titles
please visit our website or write to
the above address for a catalogue.

Bloodaxe Books Ltd acknowledges
the financial assistance of
Arts Council England, North East.

Cover printing by J. Thomson Colour Printers Ltd, Glasgow.

Printed in Great Britain by
Bell & Bain Limited, Glasgow, Scotland.

CONTENTS

ACKNOWLEDGEMENTS

Thanks to Northern Arts (Arts Council England) for sending me to the Fine Arts Work Center in Provincetown, Massachusetts, in 1997 for a month, where I was able to start work on Lady Mary Wortley Montagu. Also to Hawthornden for a Fellowship in 1999 to take it further.

Over the seven years I spent researching and writing this book I benefited from the comments and support of Andrea Badenoch, Julia Darling, Cynthia Fuller, Isobel Grundy, Jackie Hardy, Penelope Scambly Schott, Henry Shukman, Subhadassi, Debbie Taylor and Margaret Wilkinson. Many thanks to them all.

My main source was Lady Mary's letters: *Lady Mary Wortley Montagu: Letters* (Everyman, 1906), *The Complete Letters of Lady Mary Wortley Montagu*, ed. Robert Halsband (Clarendon Press 1965), *The Turkish Embassy Letters*, ed. Malcolm Jack (Virago, 1994). I am also indebted to *Lady Mary Wortley Montagu: Essays and Poems and 'Simplicity', a Comedy*, ed. Robert Halsband and Isobel Grundy (Clarendon Press, 1993), and Halsband's *The Life of Lady Mary Wortley Montagu* (Clarendon Press, 1956). The publication of Isobel Grundy's excellent biography *Lady Mary Wortley Montagu: Comet of the Enlightenment* (Oxford University Press, 1999), came at just the right time and proved invaluable. Readers of these works will hear echoes of Lady Mary's own words in my poems: it is Lady Mary herself who must be thanked for being such a delightful and illuminating Muse.

A Biographer Salutes a Poet

Who would have thought you could catch a person, a lifetime, in about sixty poems? Lots of people have tried, as I have, to write the life of Lady Mary Wortley Montagu and have been left feeling that she has somehow slipped out of the frame. She wears too many masks, plays too many roles: as rebel, flamboyant risk-taker, grist to the gossips, medical pioneer, lover, mother, contender in the lists of fame, or as Stoic, solitary, and self-sufficient.

Now Linda France has written a wonderful sequence of poems about her, which tries to catch her, and tries at the same time to let her float free. Each poem addresses a moment, offers a piercing insight, opens a window and leaves the different possibilities blowing through. The "chapter" which introduces each group of poems makes no attempt to thread them on a string or to fill in the background. It just tells you where you are, when you are, before the poems begin.

In the first poem of all Lady Mary is 'you', a little girl at her moment of triumph, addressed by an adult who understands and is moved by 'your glossy mane, your fine feathers – / the winged horse you are, exotic / and full of longing, primed / for galloping flight'. In the next, Lady Mary begins to speak as 'I' – and already speaks of the construction of self, as memory picks a past moment to hold and remember in the future. In 'Two Women' (which begins, 'There are always at least two of us') this speaker considers her two incompatible aspects, the studious self and the party self, who 'meet only on the page'.

So one of the themes of these poems is soul-building. Linda France must have steeped herself in Montagu's writings as well as in writing about her. She has entered deeply into that mysterious consciousness offered in the written words of another person, so that her poems seem astonishingly, miraculously right not only for particular episodes, particular anecdotes, but for a reader's perceptions of that earlier poet's mind and heart.

A poem called 'When in Rome', for instance, catches Lady Mary in hopeless middle-aged love, walking in the gardens of the Eternal City: 'Every night I walk in a new garden / and every night I'm sad as Tantalus. / Living with beauty is unbearable / as not living with beauty.' These lines could refer just as well to any one of a dozen other moments in Lady Mary's story; they seem to gather those moments together, in the way one's own mind moves in its constant knitting of present to past.

The level of historical accuracy, the command of detail, is excellent. Linda France has made terrific use of several facts not known before my biography. Her last poem closes on the butterfly ring that Lady Mary gave to Joshua Reynolds in her last days; and that exquisite, filigree, lost little object is transmuted here to a new beautiful object, the poem. But she also feels free to write about myth and legend as well as reliable anecdote, and proves herself capable of transmuting base metal into gold.

It's a strange experience to see one or two of my own words, along with words from Montagu, in some of these poems. It's reassuring and delightful to have been heard and understood, deeply exciting to see my own insights shifted or transfigured, humbling to see how a new reading can make the old one inadequate on its own. I'd like to think that if my biography is still around for people to buy, some will now buy it as a package with this volume of poems.

Such literate poems! With a wholly modern sensibility, they re-animate the eighteenth-century habit of allusion: not merely quoting or echoing, but waving a wand and making a new poem of the former substance. France's allusions are funny as well as stunning. Watch any eighteenth-century scholar – better yet, any female eighteenth-century scholar – hug herself and chortle over the poems addressed to Alexander Pope.

It is hard for me to judge these poems objectively. I love the woman they are written about, and I find this tribute from one writer to another both dazzling and moving. What will they be to readers who come to them cold, knowing nothing and caring nothing for Lady Mary Wortley Montagu or the eighteenth century? Only time and readers can tell, but I believe that these are exciting and memorable poems for any reader, under any conditions. Linda France has fine work already in print, but it seems to me that this sequence is her best yet. Let us hope for many readers to taste these poems and put them to the test.

ISOBEL GRUNDY

CHRONOLOGY

1689	Birth of Mary Pierrepont
1690	Her father, Evelyn Pierrepont, made Earl of Kingston. His daughter Mary titled Lady Mary Pierrepont. Birth of sister, Frances Pierrepont.
1692	Birth of brother, William.
1693	Death of her mother, Lady Mary Fielding.
1699	Death of her paternal grandmother, Elizabeth Pierrepont.
1706	Her father becomes the Marquis of Dorchester.
1712	Elopes and marries Edward Wortley Montagu.
1713	Birth of the Montagu's son, Edward Wortley Montagu. Her brother dies from smallpox.
1714	Death of Queen Anne. The Elector of Hanover proclaimed King George I. Edward Wortley Montagu elected to Parliament. Appointed Junior Commissioner by Lord Halifax.
1715	Lady Mary takes up residence in London. She contracts smallpox.
1716	*Town Eclogues* (with Pope and Gay) and *Court Poems by a Lady of Quality* published. Wortley Montagu appointed Ambassador to the Court of Turkey.
1717	Arrival in Constantinople.
1718	Birth of the Montagus' daughter Mary. Wortley Montagu recalled to England.
1719	Lady Mary takes up residence in Twickenham.
1720	*Verses written in the Chiosk of the British Palace* published.
1721	Lady Mary has her daughter inoculated publicly against smallpox.
1722	*A Plain Account of the Innoculating of the Small Pox by a Turkey Merchant* published.
1726	Her essay 'On the Mischief of Giving Fortunes with Women in Marriage' published anonymously in *Curll's Miscellanea*.
1728	Attacked by Pope in verse.
1729	Lady Mary becomes guardian to her sister, the Countess of Mar.
1733	Publication of *Verses Address'd to the Imitator of the First Satire of the Second Book of Horace*.
1736	Meets Francesco Algarotti. Lady Mary's daughter marries the Earl of Bute.
1737-8	Publishes six anonymous essays as *The Nonsense of Common Sense*.
1739	Follows Algarotti to Italy and takes up residence in Venice.
1740	Visits Florence, Rome, Naples, Leghorn, Turin, Genoa, Geneva, Chambery, Lyons, Avignon.
1742-6	Lives in Avignon.
1746	Travels to Brescia, resides in Gottolengo and visits Lovere.
1756	Returns to Venice and Padua.
1758	Death of Edward Wortley Montagu. Lady Mary leaves Italy for Germany and Holland.
1762	Returns to England. Death of Lady Mary Wortley Montagu.

CHAPTER THE FIRST

In which our heroine is born Mary Pierrepont in the year
1689 to Evelyn Pierrepont and Lady Mary Fielding: the
same year William of Orange and Mary, daughter of James
II, are offered, and accept, the throne of England; the
Battle of the Boyne leaves an indelible stain on Irish soil;
while Locke writes *A Letter Concerning Toleration* and
Purcell's *Dido and Aeneas* is performed, some say for the
first time, at Mr Josias Priest's Boarding School for Girls
in Chelsea. A year, like any other year, that sees human
nature at its best and at its worst.

The following year Mary Pierrepont becomes Lady Mary
when her parents are created Earl and Countess of King-
ston. She is just three years old when her mother dies,
leaving her and her two sisters, Frances and Evelyn, and
brother William, to grow up in her paternal grandmother's
charge at West Dean, near Salisbury, and after her death,
in 1698, at the family seat, Thoresby Hall in Nottingham-
shire, as well as at their town house in London.

Although Mary's formal education is limited to the tra-
ditional feminine skills of drawing, a little Italian, embroidery
and cookery, dancing and riding, she spends more time
than is usual for a daughter in her father's library, reading
by the yard, teaching herself Latin and writing poetry,
romantic prose and confident imitations of classical texts.
When her father acquires the title Marquis of Dorchester in
1706, Mary acts as his hostess, entertaining Whig politicians
and men of letters such as Congreve, Addison and Steele.
She says later 'I came young into the hurry of the world'.

On the death of William III in 1702, Queen Anne takes
the crown, the last Stuart monarch. In the course of her life
she becomes pregnant eighteen times but no child survives.
Under the leadership of the Duke of Marlborough, England
continues to engage in the war over the question of the
Spanish Succession and the balance of power in Europe.
Defoe and Dryden, Congreve and Swift, Newton, Locke and
Astell are all making work for the new publishing houses
whose task it is to spread the written word, extending the
net of culture with not a little swagger and flourish across
Europe and beyond.

Fashions for both men and women rely on a regular haul of whalebone: to make men's coats stand out over their long waistcoats and to serve as hoops to stretch women's skirts out at the hips, draped with panniers of chintz or printed calico. Water is generally not safe to drink so most people tend to drink beer or gin. If a person is drunk they are said to be *hicksius-doxius*; if hungover they are *womblety-cropt*. They are often either one or the other. England is raising its glass to the new century, with high hopes for the blessings of Order, Justice and Prosperity.

The Toast of the Kit-Cat Club

He sets you upon the table –
a human candelabra,
the wide white shine of you
dimming the litter of crystal
and silver – your father, holding
your hand like a halter
and him the proud rider.
See all the men's faces spinning
a chart around you, grinning
and blowing like the four winds
of heaven, raising their goblets
of hock, their pipes, like trumpets,
like flags. It's all smoke and shine
and glory. Another world.
And their cheering is all for you.
You are their toast, their mascot;
your little girl's cheeks
an ecstasy of pink. They feed you
sweetmeats and titbits, stroke
your glossy mane, your fine feathers –
the winged horse you are, exotic
and full of longing, primed
for galloping flight. This is what
you want to remember, the map

you will follow: how it is
to be admired; to be good
as any man. Your father
gives you a cordial to sip.
It tastes of promise and triumph;
makes your stinging eyes weep.

Salisbury Cathedral

The faster I run
towards it the further
away the spire seems
to tower over me
and rolling chalk
and green.

It is only later
I will remember this
or going back there
and finding nothing
will tell myself
that's what I remember.

The Carving Master

Three times a week he comes to talk to me
about meat. His cheeks are pale as chicken breasts.

They shine as he tells me always to cut
against the grain, never to be mean.

He wears the rank smell of grease and gravy
as if it were French perfume. I humour him.

No fault of his I must be the butcher
at my father's carnivals; always eat

alone, before I carve a ham towards
the bone, sever pike or salmon in two;

serve the choicest cuts to the most honoured guests.
Flesh, fish and fowl, each one a different blade.

I can recite the sliced anatomy
of pigeon and woodcock, of master and maid,

like the conjugations of Latin verbs:
learn the difference between *one* and *all*.

When I take up my pen I hold it
like a knife and carve my name on the page.

Two Women

There are always at least two of us.
I like the one in the library best
because I know I can trust her, know
she is good. How I admire her fine plan
for a priory of single women,
to live and study and tend the gardens.
She would be the abbess, queen of reason.
When she is twelve, she gives up eating cakes,
reading novels at fifteen. For higher things.
That is the sort of woman she is.

I admit the one I can't resist
is her sister, the maverick who loves
to dance, the swish of petticoats, a flash
of slipper; whose eyes glitter with wine
and the whirl of pleasure; who always
has an answer, doesn't stint on laughter.
One night she loses a hundred pounds at cards;
not a blush or a blink. She is a hustler,
a pirate, actress and lover. No wonder
everyone melts in the torch of her gaze.

Two women, jasmine and jade, and I am
always there, watching them glide
between their different worlds, like day
climbing the stairs into night. The only place
they meet is on the page, the only time
that suits them both. It is a small room
full of shadows, walls papered and bloomed
with the limits of my skin, the riot of my thoughts.
They only quarrel when the door is closed;
come out smiling like angels, like tyrants.

Marriage Market

We laughed and joked
    so we wouldn't cry,
invented a code to sugar
    the lies – either
Hell or *Limbo* or *Paradise.*

While our parents plotted
    to consign us to fire,
the best we could expect
    was emptiness we'd fill
with dreams of lush green,

summer heat, dew-splashed
    blooms, perfume spicing
ripe air, rosy apples, fresh
    and sweet, hanging
from the trees, just out of reach.

In My Lady's Chamber
(for Anne Wortley Montagu)

Would you think it charming, my dear,
if I came and stole your chamberpot?
If I used it as a goblet to drink
a toast to your beauty and my love?

Or would you think it a nuisance,
when you needed it quickly
in the middle of the night
and found it gone? Would you curse me?

Already I can hear you laughing,
my dear, and that's enough of a toast –
to your beauty and my love,
an upstairs, downstairs kiss.

[18]

CHAPTER THE SECOND

In which Lady Mary attracts the attention of Edward Wortley Montagu, Whig MP for Huntingdon and brother of her close friend Anne. Their courtship is mostly conducted by letter: fickle, jealous, unlikely, more pedantic than passionate. Lady Mary's father and Edward disagree over the terms of the marriage contract: Dorchester wants a large jointure in the event of Wortley's death, with everything held in trust for the yet-to-be-born eldest son. Wortley considers this custom outdated and misguided; better to confer wealth on a son as reward for his worth rather than his age. Lady Mary herself deplores the whole idea of settlements, dowries and bartering for brides. In a dramatic sequence of missed trysts and undercover journeys, Edward and Mary elope together.

They begin married life moving between London and Sheffield and York, often separately, while Edward attends to business in his constituency. Nine months after their marriage a son, Edward, is born. Two months later Lady Mary's brother, William, Lord Kingston, dies of small-pox, leaving a widow in her teens and two small children.

Lady Mary, reconciled with her father, is Toast of the Whig Hanover Club. In 1714 she anonymously publishes a satirical essay on marriage in the *Spectator*. In law it is an unequal partnership: if a man murders his wife, he would be hanged for felony; if a woman murders her husband, she is committing treason and so would be burned alive.

Queen Anne dies and the Hanoverian Succession is secured with the Accession of George I.

Letters to Edward

March 1710

This thing you call Love – we must've been reading
different books. Mine are all on the same shelf

as Nature and Truth. Listen: I wouldn't lie
to myself so how could I lie to you?

I could change the weather of your days
but you'd still need to watch the horizon for storms.

Why are clever men so foolish?
If you don't trust me, that's a disease

I'd rather not be infected by.
I'll just imagine you burning this letter,

watching black words blacken into ash.
Enjoy it – it'll be the last you get.

And I'm not a woman to change her mind.

*

April

Not one but two letters where I expected
silence – and in both what a strange picture

you paint of me: I am neither that good
nor that bad. You would be disappointed

twice. Maybe you should save yourself the trouble.
I can't say I could ever love you.

I could admire you, be your friend. This Love
is a dish I've never tasted. How

do I know if I'll like it? And how

do I know you are not prone to greed

so once you've eaten your fill you'll rise
from the table, fat and sick of the sight

of food? What if I'm left to dine alone?

*

August – November

Love is love and money is money.
I can promise you neither. How much plainer

can I be? If you'd stop expecting me
to act like a woman, we might find

we chime instead of clash. I will not sing
out of tune and I'll not be despised for it.

You know I have no power in the world.
To be a woman is to be a slave.

If I'm not my own keeper, at least
let me set the price of my own soul, dearer

to me than all the church bells in London,
all my father's land, his property.

My name is etched on his inventory.

*

Admit it: you're enjoying this drama,
this pantomime of flaming hoops and horses,

with you the ringmaster, cracking his whip.
You've cast me in the wrong part. I'm no clown,

no acrobat. You'll never bruise my sturdy heart.
This bull is not for baiting. If I wear

a gold ring I'll not be led by it;
I'll never be so dazzled by its shine

I can't see the road in front of me, how
straight it is, taking me where I want to go.

Not this wheeling round and round in circles,
the sting of the leather, your painted smile.

Tell me: don't we both know the show's over?

*

Spring 1711

I read too many romances when I was young.
I thought we were one – a happy ending.

If I'd dreamt about clothes and balls and coaches,
perhaps they would have come true. Unlike you.

I have a dream of friendship too – as close
as eyelashes brushed together in sleep,

a shared view of the world wide awake.
An intimacy that blooms with time, sets

seed and never dies. Could we rise to that?
I think this is what men call surrender.

Believe the white flag of its innocence.
I need you, want you more than Marlborough

burned to win his battle at Blenheim.

*

July 1712

There is no war worse than between father
and child. He keeps me prisoner. I'm laced

with scars but he won't break my spirit
with his old man's ideas about settlements.

If I can't marry for love, I won't marry
at all. I told Clotworthy-Skeffington

as much (*imagine being shackled
to such a name!*) and he said he'd teach me

obedience. I am twenty-three years old
and everyone treats me like a child.

I have no inheritance, no liberty.
And now I think I have no father.

No grace, no fortune, no lover either.

*

August

What you see is what you get – just me;
nothing but a nightgown and a petticoat

to my name. You won't regret it. Be content.
You can be pleased with nothing when you are

not pleased with yourself. You must beware
of gravity and I of levity:

together we'll balance the scales. Naples
perhaps – somewhere novel and beautiful

so we won't run out of things to say.
I want this to be forever. I sweat

at the thought of its beginning, its ending,
the danger of my own heart's desires.

I am yours. Love me and use me well.

*

October – November

The words of a wife are new to me, catch
in my throat like fish bones; this distance

between us. I miss you. I want to drink
the words of a husband like soup to comfort me.

But no word comes. Have you no desire
to write my name now that it is your own?

I lie awake at night and imagine
accidents, count them like milestones on the road

between us. All I want is to climb into
a sulkie and race to where you are,

as my blood races, the beat of my lonely heart.
A robin keeps me company.

We sing to each other and compare crimsons.

*

1712–13

Too much time alone is making me sour
as a windfall plum. I want to stay young,

to ripen in the ignorance of hope.
I never wanted to grow as wise as this,

seduced by the lure of a dull eye,
a jaded appetite. I am a machine

for writing, reading, walking and sleeping,
a voyeur of other people's foibles.

Every thought I have comes back to you.
What would Edward say? What would Edward do?

I'm a candle guttering in the draught.
I want you to come home and close the door

behind you; let my flame be still again, rise.

*
1714

Your letters are rare as snow in summer,
as cold. They numb where they should melt. I want you

to miss me as much as I miss you.
Your blank pages, this long emptiness

are so many arrows I pluck from my flesh;
feel the sting of my wounds, your salty words.

I'm turning into a pietà of stone.
If not for me, have you no tenderness

for your son, your own sinew and bone?
If not with us, where is your passion's home?

I want no more letters written on glass.
The next you send I will shatter; return

each crystal wrapped in white paper, my tears.

'The first year I was married'

I looked in all those books I read
as if they were mirrors. And my eyes
flashed back their dazzle of ideas
about Love and Beauty and Truth
till I was half-blind in the light,
the heat. How much I wanted
reason and rhythm to hold, to thrill.
My virgin white. I wrote extempore
on a windowpane, a diamond
for a quill – lines I found inside
my heart about truth, transparent as glass
I could see my own face in at last.

Chapter the Third

In which Lady Mary joins her husband in London to support his political career and win favour at the Court of George I, whom she considered 'an honest blockhead'. Her father is made Duke of Kingston and later Lord Privy Seal. Alexander Pope becomes a friend and collaborates with Lady Mary and John Gay on a series of satirical poems, one for each day of the week, known as the *Town Eclogues*. These are published in a pirated edition by Edmund Curll. Even though Curll only refers to Lady Mary as 'a Lady of Quality', the fact of her authorship is common enough knowledge. A woman writing and being published is contrary to the dictates of contemporary protocol, an offence to Fashion and Society; an *aristocratic* woman writing and being published doubly so.

Her sister's husband, Lord Mar, is an activist in the Jacobite Rebellion and after its failure, leaves for France with the Pretender to the throne, James II's son.

A particularly violent strain of smallpox is sweeping through London and Lady Mary is one of the unfortunates infected by it. The early stages are marked by a high fever and severe pains in the head, back and muscles. A common treatment is to drape the patient's chamber with bright red fabric to draw out the infection. As this is of little assistance many victims die from haemorrhages in the lungs or elsewhere even before the appearance of the rash, pimples growing into large itchy pustules, often colonising the whole body. Once the fever breaks, the scabs fall away after a few weeks, leaving life-long scars. This leads to a fashion for patches, red or black silk cut into circles or crescents, stuck onto the face, preferably painted with white lead, to hide the pockmarks. Lady Mary, famous for her beauty and in particular her striking dark eyes, is left with a scarred complexion and no eyelashes.

Morning

Maybe I'll wake up alone and make rays
of my arms and legs across the buttercup
silk of my big meadow bed; their sleepy heat,
that no man's land, before day's urgency
lifts me into its coolness. I listen
to Duke Street struggling into its rumpled breeches
outside my window, pulling on its three-cornered hat
and writing its name on the top of the day.
I keep to the corners of my counterpane
and read the latest pearls, the sharpest knives.
Who thinks what? And do I agree? My mind
is widest when I'm lying down. I scribble
in the margins.
                 At eleven o'clock
my maid brings me a cup of chocolate
and my son comes to play hide and seek
in my curtains. The odd words his fat cheeks make
bubble and pop but we string together
a bracelet of *Mama* and *boat* and *ball*.
Bye bye, baby. The girl will help me dress.
My whalebone silhouette. A holding of breath.
I paint a picture in blue brocade,
cream chintz; hang jewels in all the right places,
powder my face just enough to show I care,
dress my hair into glossy perfect folds.
The morning has made me its favourite,
its freshest publication, my ink still wet.

Some Nights

I take off my clothes like a cherry tree
shedding its petals, just letting them fall.
Edward leaves his glass of port half-drunk
on the table and comes to me, heavy
with wanting, and warm; his breath in my ear.

Almanac

A comet, a total eclipse of the sun
and the northern lights – sky's signs
of fire in the blood, the drawing
of swords – seeds of a sister's war.

The river thickened to a road of ice –
a mirror for roasting oxen on –
the city, lost, white and surprised
by the tight cold of its own fear.

Poles of fire and ice, north and south,
day and night – as they spin and confound
the world so they also wheel within.

An early sign of fever is shivering.

Pox

Whose idea was it to call it small?
Small as the ocean. Small as the world.
I don't want to be a citizen of its flesh.
I don't want to sing its anthems of pustules and fever.

I don't want to feel this hot, this cold.
I don't want to be plagued with this aching.
My body's too big for my skin. I don't want to burst.
I don't want to stew in the seeping of my own flesh.

I don't want to dream of graveyards, nights so dark
with the dust of wild horses, their hooves bruising moons
all over me. I don't want morning to come
like a torch on the wall, smudges of shadows
and no one there. I don't want to be a house on fire.

I don't want eyelids pink and smooth as seashells,
face pitted as a peachstone. I don't want to paint
over the cracks with white lead, its tang of blood.
I don't want to be a cypher, a worn-out patch, a cloud
of powder. I don't want to stop wearing feathers in my hair.

I don't want to be anybody's patient.
I don't want to play Hazard with angels.
I don't want to be a book written by someone else.
I won't have anything to do with anything small.

Like a Phoenix

For two months I lived a dream
of death under the constellation Pox.

And when I awoke I bore its brand
on my face, a rash of empty white stars,

a snappishness in my lashless eyes.
Now I was nobody's child. I'd seen

the blackness at the edge of the sky,
in the hollow of my own heart.

Nowhere answered to the name of home.
I surrendered to the luck of the living,

the fall of the dice, the right word
at the right time. Edward whispered *East*

in my ear like a lemon-scented breeze
and I was an arrow angling for air,

for the sheer joy of flight, of stretching
the compass of my flaming wings.

CHAPTER THE FOURTH

In which Edward Wortley Montagu is appointed Ambassador to the Court of Turkey and the whole family and their entourage travel overland to Constantinople, calling in at the Courts of Hanover and Vienna, through Belgrade, Sophia and Adrianople. Lady Mary writes home: 'I have long learnt to hold myself as nothing, but when I think of the fatigue my poor infant must suffer, I have all a mother's fondness in my eyes, and all her tender passions in my heart.'

Witnessing the Turkish custom of inoculation against smallpox, Lady Mary has the operation performed on her son. Her daughter, Mary, is born in Constantinople, not 'one of my diverting adventures, though I must own that it is not half so mortifying here as in England, there being as much difference as there is between a little cold in the head, which sometimes happens here, and the consumptive coughs in London...Nobody keeps to their house a month for lying in and I am not so fond of any of our customs to retain them when they are not necessary.'

She writes copious letters and a journal describing her experiences and rehearsing her opinions of all the different cultures she is exposed to: these form the core of the posthumously published *Embassy Letters*. She comes to the conclusion that 'the manners of mankind do not differ so widely as our voyage writers would make us believe'. After meeting Nicolas-Francois Rémond in Paris, he begins writing her a series of increasingly unwelcome letters, flattering Lady Mary as well as himself.

Wortley Montagu's mission to engineer some sort of peace between the Austro-Hungarian and the Ottoman Empires fails and he is recalled to England in 1718. They return home by sea and land, via North Africa, where they visit the ancient city of Carthage, and Genoa and Turin, over Mount Cenis to Lyons and Paris. Here Lady Mary meets her sister, Frances, on her way to join Lord Mar in exile.

Through the Netherlands

Crossing the water was a long sleep,
stillness and storms; waking up,
land's insistence to be itself.

The light plays tricks – what once
was familiar as flesh peels back
in layers of varnish and oils.

Even the air has a different smell,
foreign as the flat landscape
of words swallowed and spat.

I am sprung from my mother's root,
walking in a country that is blossom and branch,
a garden to lose tomorrow in, the past.

The yews are cups of coolness,
keeping the secret of their dark,
every arbour another threshold.

On the Road

Rotterdam Nijmegen Reinburg Stamel
Cologne Frankfurt Vienna Leipzig Prague

The carriage wheels rattle with their names,
singing the map of them, stirring the dust of them.
I'm hungry and dirty, battered and bruised,
but I'm writing letters in my head on the road.

To Lady Mar Sarah Chiswell Lady Bristol Lady Rich
To Anne Thistlethwayte Alexander Pope

And I love this gypsy life, this never knowing
how or where a day will end. I could be
a paultrie peddlar, a footpad cloaked in black,
brazen as vengeance, free as kindness.

Brunswick Hanover Blankenburg Vienna
Hernhausen Buda Peterwardein Belgrade

My Lovely Empress
(for Elisabeth Christine, at the court of Charles VI in Vienna)

You watch me as a child plays with a friend,
your laughing eyes daring me to resist
your charms.
                    How could I? Did Paris
see Helen, turn his back and walk away?
Was Aphrodite a lonely woman?
Did Dido freeze?
                    I dream of your sweet mouth,
that fine white hand you hold out to be kissed.
Someone else's happiness. Even jealous
of the cards you hold when you're playing quinze.

Teach me how to gamble with your grace.
How to hold a gun, hit the target
wreathed with the motto *Here is no shame*
to the vanquished, true as Cupid's aim.

I'll forget to mention this. Just keep
your picture where I can see it, set in diamonds.

First Fruit

It's
a Chinese pagoda,
a garden jester,
a creature from the sea,
a mountebank's wigstand,
a pirate's treasure,
a bee's nest,
a puzzle tree.

On the King's table with lemons and oranges,
its name is pineapple, *ananas*. Cut off
its head, it doesn't bleed. Crocodile gourd
full of sun. Its gold shames all the other fruit
to pitch. Smell its freshness. Suck the shock
of its sweet meat. Bite. Acid burst on your tongue,
dribble of juice down your chin, fibre thresh
between your teeth. Your eyes grow sharp
as sovereigns; your mouth shining
like a Midas kiss, eating Brazil in Germany.

'How agreeably the time slides away with me'
Vienna, Autumn 1716

Every day is a gala day, ombre
and piquet, cards as crisp as the talk is,
as sharp and tinkling as the ice is – all
we eat – the percussion of spoons,
the clink of our crystal, wine from Lorraine.

I am a lodestone, drawing all the world
into my field – a mosaic of gold,
an emerald as big as a teacup,
lapis lazuli, a clockwork crawfish,
enormous agates, hallfuls of treasure.

I'm breathing a scene by Correggio
or Titian, drinking toasts to the Emperor
and his best crucifix, the fine women
with their black hair, beautiful as waxworks,
in danger of melting too close to the fire.

I stay warm by the stoves I will install
for myself in England, listening to horns,
swallowing oysters. My best friends are Spanish,
elegant and shameless. I won't go home;
not while there's still this singing, this dancing.

Border Country
The Battlefield at Peterwardein

This place is a wasteland,
heartless and cold. Only the wind
keens for the unburied dead.

Here is a lost city,
stones telling the old story
of murder posing as glory.

Virgin earth bears the scar
of good men seduced by war,
trumpeting their true nature.

The plains are shrouded in snow,
pocked with stunted trees, so
many flocks of birds, dead men's souls.

Crossing the Alps
(after Orpheus)

Let me die a poet's death.

Let me drown in a fast foreign river,
calling the name of my true love
as the current sweeps me away.

Let me die a poet's death.

Let me hear the dark leaves on the trees
calling the name of my true love,
the whispering echo of my last breath.

Let me die a poet's death.

Let men sing of how I drowned
calling the name of my true love.
Crown me with laurels, carve me in stone.

But let me die a poet's death.

Adrianople, April

I'm living in a zoo with tulips.
Trajan's Gate keeps the cages closed. They toss
the severed heads and hands and feet of fools
over the parapet to feed the creatures
of the night. It's too hot to move.
We languish in the seraglio,
drinking coffee and sherbet, lounging
on cushions and magic carpets,
listening to the gossip of fountains.
The women stroke my cheek and coo
Üzelle, pek üzelle. But I'm in love
with my fine white horse, her black eyes.

I'm having a picnic in Paradise,
collecting travellers' tales like a miser
hoarding gold. I count coins in my sleep,
stack fat towers of teeth money, the cost
of biting this city to pieces. Each year
the storks make their pilgrimages to Mecca.
I am blessed: they protect my house
against pestilence and fire, the horned demons
of buffaloes with their maggotty eyes,
their bloody brows. I swathe
myself in a ferace when I visit
the Jew's shop where lovers meet in secret.

I am a pioneer, the first Christian
to make this journey in a hundred years.
I deserve to wear a cloak of the fur
of the black muscovite fox, a kalpak
studded with jonquils and jasmine. I have seen
a century of camels roped together
in the desert. This could be the *Iliad*:
the women weave their stories in the shade,
dance like Diana in the moonlight.
And I dance too. Wherever you live
you take yourself with you, your own cage.
I am a zoo, a garden of tulips.

In the Bagnio

The first thing you think of is corsets.

If you don't take them off, you will suffer.
And you will surely suffer if you do.
You are from England, a green country
where only horses sweat. Here the air's thick
as mare's breath and no one frets
about nakedness. The sulphurous steam
draws all your troubles out through your pores.
The women shine and glide, so many daughters
of Eve, Venuses fresh from the foam;
glowing proof that if the fashion decreed
we must all go naked, no one would name
a pretty face. A man would give his last dinar
to be a fly on these tingling marble walls.
If he crossed the threshold, he'd lose his head.
The women are free to bathe and gossip,
braid each other's hair, sip coffee
or sherbet, dabble in the sun-splashed fountains.
Everything is luxury; everything is gorgeous.

And the last thing you think of is corsets.

Incognito

My dear, you would hardly know me – all dressed
up in my caftan and drawers, damask rose
brocaded with silver, diamonds on my breast.

I've cast off all my English wigs and bows;
gone Turkish, my hair pearl and ribbon-tressed,
white kid slippers spun with gold on my toes.

Heron's feathers nod from the velvet nest
of my cap. A crescent wing of jewels shows
my bare neck at its milky opal best.

I clasp my belt of satin and stones close
with a cluster of sparkling diamonds. Lest
it's cold, I drape myself in sable throws.

The women here are beautiful and blessed.
With soft kohl they paint their eyes black as does';
go out in long veils – nothing to suggest

who or how many are meeting their beaux.
Here we all go incognito. East, west,
a woman will reap the secrets she sews.

Recipe to Prevent the Smallpox

September is the month of blood and nutshells
when the old woman will come with her needle.

The old woman will come with her hollow shell
seeking the veins in your arms and your legs.

She will scratch them open with her silver needle,
the old woman who will come with her shellful

of smallpox and stitch pinpricks of pox
into the veins of your arms and your legs,

binding them tight with a patch of hollow shell.
The old woman will go about her business

and on the eighth day you will take to your bed
with a fever. You will take to your bed

and your face will erupt in running sores.
Two days on you will be well again, free

from distemper. Two years on you will take
the recipe home although no one will trust it.

No one will trust the month of blood and nutshells
when the English lady comes with her needle.

Dear England

Every day I'm looking for a letter,
a small white square of home I'll hold up to
the gilt-framed window to read it better.
I write too many. I receive too few.

Tell me all the scandal, the latest news.
And how you languish, missing the pleasure
of my laughter, my talent to amuse;
how England's lost its most precious treasure.

I yearn for strokes of a familiar hand,
a page of tender phrases, to remind
me of friends I miss in that far-off land
I'm missing too. I want it to be signed

with the blush and flourish of your name.
And, my dearest, I will send you the same.

CHAPTER THE FIFTH

In which Lady Mary becomes a leading figure in London literary life and is fêted as a wit and intellectual. Pope is particularly lavish in his attentions. Lady Mary says 'What a goddess he made of me…' Her letter from Constantinople to the Abbé Conti is published without her permission. *Verses Written in the Chiosk of the British Palace* also appears. It is a fruitful, argumentative time for literature, with Defoe's *Robinson Crusoe* and *Moll Flanders*, Pope's *Dunciad*, Swift's *Gulliver's Travels* and Gay's *Beggar's Opera*.

Sir Robert Walpole, championed by Lady Mary, is at the height of his powers as Britain's first and longest-serving Prime Minister. George II takes over from his father on 11 October 1727.

Lady Mary's star begins to wane when she is blackmailed by Rémond, on whose behalf she had unsuccessfully speculated in the South Sea Company, encouraged by Pope and 'the scent of money…in the air like the breath of spring'. The Bubble bursts in 1720, leaving many investors and bankers poor and red-faced. She begins campaigning for inoculation against smallpox and has the operation performed on her daughter. The medical profession discredit and humiliate her. Incognito she sends *A Plain Account of the Inoculating of the Small Pox by a Turkey Merchant* to 'The Flying Post'. She writes an essay on marriage in the style of Rochefoucault and enjoys meeting Voltaire. She also acts as patron to her second cousin, Henry Fielding.

As Lady Mary's friendship with Pope cools, other friendships with Lord Hervey and Maria Skerrett, Walpole's mistress, deepen. Her father and her younger sister, Evelyn, Lady Gower, die. Her son runs away from school to sea. His parents decide to keep him abroad to complete his education. Family life is consistently fraught: Lady Mary fights for and wins the legal and financial battle for custody of her now mentally ill sister, Lady Mar. Her son returns to England without permission to claim his legacies and his parents order him back. Lady Mary is attacked by Pope in verse and, with Lord Hervey, retaliates in *Verses Address'd to the Imitator of Horace*. The feud continues. Under all these various strains, Lady Mary weakens and falls ill.

True Likeness

All my portraits show a different woman.
Not only her clothes or the way she stands.
Not just this one blue, this one cinnamon,
or a slip of the painter's clumsy hands.

My body is classical, Protean,
blessed with that sea god's gift of prophecy,
of shifting-shape, untamed, chameleon.
More for its own sake, for Art's, than secrecy.

Some details prevail – my cinched waist, small feet
in pointed slippers. They're just fashion's lie.
Not the fire you'll maybe catch in the heat
of what some call my wild and staring eye.

If you see me, in cinnamon or blue,
look hard. Tell me which one you think is true.

To the Imitator of Horace
(Mr Alexander Pope)

I

You dreamed you'd cast a statue of my soul;
desired me naked, an empty white page
to illuminate with girlish dimples,
eyes like the moon. You were Pygmalion,
God, Mr Taste.
                              Across all of Europe
you undressed me, unlacing my layers
with every letter, painting on fresh coats
of gilt. Day after day I became more
divine, an alphabet to your design.
Your breath blew hump-backed up the Bosphorus
and spouted bed-time stories in my ear.

It was your mind's mirror that I aspired
to stand like Eve in. Why didn't you guess
that I could not be pressed in copper, bronze
or airy nothingness; would not be dressed
in anyone's gold but my own?

                                   Dear Pope,
of all my friends, you should have known me well
enough: that if I were the moon on fire
in any man's eyes, I'd wear the disguise
of Diana, the hunter not the prey.
Between the two of us – my arrows, her aim –
we'd strike that graven clay by lightning; watch
it crack and blow its dust away like snuff.

II

I fell in love with Savile House, the place
you found for me next door to you; a house
handsome and convenient, bricks and slates
I could trust. That balmy summer greened me
into a gardener. When I'd had enough
of earth, I'd walk down to the river, to you.

You wanted me to hang in your best room,
you said, that way you'd keep the wanderer
at home. Constantinople behind me,
I'd watch Father Thames galloping eastwards
before me. Framed in silence, pantalooned,
how could I ever look you straight in the eye?

My favourite room was the gallery
where we shared out the harpsichord like cake;
sweeter tunes to my good ear than the sharps
and flats of those black puns you couldn't give up
if you tried. How stop a river flowing
through a city to reach its mother, the sea?

III

If a man were to write a love poem
for one woman and then, later, send it
to another;

                              if he were to pay them
both the same compliment and say they were
like the moon (which, on the whole, he preferred
to women);

                              if he were only up to
dipping his quill into ink pots he stole
and spilled, then forgot –

                              tell me,
                                        would you buy
a second-hand carriage from such a man?
Would you consider marriage?

IV

What dire offence from amorous causes springs.
What mighty contests rise from trivial things.

A Short List of Amorous Causes:

- Using the moon for your own ends
- Being jealous of my good friends
- Going on and on about sex
- Acting like a cringing reject
- Too much doubt of your own power
- Too much acid turned you sour

A Short List of Trivial Things:

– Mixing with spies, turncoats and cheats
– Saying I soiled your blessed sheets
– Wanting everyone to conform
  to your own coarse and twisted norm
– Blinded by the sun in my eye
– Sooner be a dog than let it lie

Who's to really say which is which?
Pope the dog thought I was a bitch.

My Lord Hervey and I and the Colour Green

We disagree about green.
He doesn't believe in it.
Thinks the countryside evil.
Won't be seen dead in pea,
olive or leek, grass or leaf.

*

At Heidegger's masquerades
I always recognise him
despite his disguise, the frills
around his eyes. You can't hide
the rub of the green, stray signs
of fortune, a gentleman
of the green baize road.

*

With him I am a woman
drunk on her own words – chartreuse,
viridian, Paris green.

*

It's clear he thinks my veins flow
with chlorophyll, my heart beats
green with greed. He tells me what
nature makes nature will take
care of. If green's the colour
of Venus and Spring and Faith,
let me believe, surrender.

*

When he leaves with the same man
I've been flirting with all night,
I hardly notice the sting
of that monster, the colour
of its eyes we never name.

*

For him I shed my fig leaf,
reveal my secrets. We eat
green apples in the sun. Risk
the hazard of knowledge. Trust
in the poison and the cure.

*

The world's full of many things
but it's fuelled by men, women,
Herveys and the colour green.

CHAPTER THE SIXTH

In which Lady Mary meets and falls in love with a 24 year-old bisexual poet and scientist from Italy, Count Francesco Algarotti. She competes shamelessly with Lord Hervey for his affection.

Anonymously she publishes *The Nonsense of Common Sense*, a pro-Walpole and Whig paper that runs to nine issues 'as long as the Author thinks fit, and the Publick likes it'. She covers such topics as encouraging the native woollen trade, lowering interest rates, reducing the wastefulness and ostentation of various assemblies, banishing corruption and malpractice within the publishing business and a defence of women: 'A woman really virtuous in the utmost extent of this expression has virtue of a purer kind than any philosopher has ever shewn, since she knows if she has Sense (and without it there can be no Virtue) that Mankind is too much prejudice'd against her Sex to give her any Degree of that Fame which is so sharp a spur to their Greatest Actions...Begin then Ladies by paying those Authors with Scorn and contempt who with the sneer of affected Admiration would throw you below the Dignity of the Human Species.'

Lady Mary's daughter marries the Earl of Bute and her niece demands custody of Lady Mar. Two of her closest friends die, Maria Skerrett and Lady Stafford. In the hope of improving her health and spirits (and of living with Algarotti in Venice), Lady Mary prepares to leave England. Walpole's power is being eroded and Britain and Spain are at war.

Chimera

(for Francesco Algarotti)

Chimera.
1. A fire-breathing monster, with a lion's head, a goat's body, and a serpent's tail, killed by Bellerophon.
2. A grotesque monster.
3. A mere wild fancy; an unfounded conception.

My love for you breathes fire, speaks in tongues
of flame, a blaze that keeps me warm and burns
me. I can only utter it in French.

It has a lion's head, majestic, proud.
Its throne is the sun, my sky, my centre.
I count the gold of its brazen roaring.

Its body belongs to a goat, famous
for wild lustiness, sturdy with longing.
This one climbs the highest, lasts the longest.

The end of it's a serpent's tail, the whip
of distance, the sting of indifference.
It flays you naked; a dream of dying.

What creature stalks the chambers of my heart?
Perhaps my own invention; not a monster.
Just a single flame that needs air to burn.

On Air and Absence
(for F.A.)

Away from you, I'm a bird in a jar,
burnt mercury in a vessel of glass –

an experiment in pain. I am a magnet
smashed in a thousand pieces,

its poles lost, pushing and falling,
falling away. My mouth is full of earth;

every day a lesson in gravity. No entry
under *Flight*. I am a flame trapped

in a treatise on the nature of time
and the elements. One minute, you're there

in more than three dimensions; the next,
not even a puff of smoke, the smallest drop

of salty water. Not even thin air.
I make a table of your absence; mark

the numbers, the colour of the days.
But it needs more than science, love,

to prove how long it will be before
we meet, before I can breathe again.

My Little Thread Satin Beauty
(for Molly Skerrett)
1738

When I listed the qualities of desire,
what a woman should look for in a lover,
I was writing a map of our friendship.

For weren't we lost in the sheer joy of it,
that paradise of champagne and chicken,
Athene and Venus, hand in glove?

You sang all my lions and tigers to sleep;
patrolled the wildest boroughs of my heart.
You were the child and you mothered me.

Astonishing, impossible creature,
you loved who you liked and liked who you loved;
your name, a kiss my lips never tired of.

The year you died the world caught fire; all the words
we shared, blood and bone, flaming. Who can read
the future in silver ash? Who can tell

whether I will find in my lover such
balance and beauty, such kindness, all the gifts
you held in your small and lovely hands, my friend?

Or if I'll harden into bark or thin
into the chill transparency of river
so I won't know myself, always alone,

without you – the terror and the pity –
Molly, my little thread satin beauty?

What to Take with You

13 trunks and cases, all monogrammed
3 boxes of books (687 catalogued)
A box of hats, black and green velvet
3 shagreen jewel-cases
A hair trunk of sundry clothes
1 scarlet dress from Turkey
20 pieces of Turkish caffoy (formerly cushion cases)
Workbox with embroidery, worsteds and chintz
1 side-saddle and riding gear
Box of china
A Turkish knife
4 chairs
Bureau (and papers)
Japanned cabinet (and letters)
Small bookcase
Large box of snuff
Confidence of a true believer
Clear conscience
Faith and hope
Eclipse of the sun
Map of Elysium

CHAPTER THE SEVENTH

In which Lady Mary crosses the Channel and travels through France and across the Alps to Venice with a prodigious amount of baggage. Algarotti has meanwhile become the favourite of Frederick II at the Prussian Court and loiters there, reluctant to join her. Lady Mary makes a tour of Italy.

She comes across Horace Walpole and Thomas Gray in Venice. Walpole reports his impressions of her in letters home: '…a third she-meteor. Those learned luminaries the Ladies Pomfret and Walpole are to be joined by the Lady Mary Wortley Montagu. You have not been witness to the rhapsody of mystic nonsense which these two fair ones debate incessantly, and consequently cannot figure what must be the issue of this triple alliance…Only figure the coalition of prudery, debauchery, sentiment, history, Greek, Latin, French, Italian, and metaphysics; all, except the second understood by halves, by quarters, or not at all… She laughs at my Lady Walpole, scolds my Lady Pomfret, and is laughed at by the whole town. Her dress, her avarice, and her impudence must amaze any one that never heard her name. She wears a foul mob, that does not cover her greasy black locks, that hang loose, never combed or curled; an old mazarine blue wrapper, that gapes open and dis-covers a canvas petticoat. Her face swelled violently on one side with a — [*pox*], partly covered with a plaister, and partly with white paint, which for cheapness she has bought so coarse, that you should not use it to wash a chimney…often mentioned in Mr Pope's Works, and famous for her Wit, Poems, Intrigues, Avarice, and Dirt.'

All Lady Mary writes of their meeting is: 'Hory was… particularly civil.' One of them is lying.

Lady Mary and Algarotti eventually manage to spend two months together in Turin, 'a most disagreeable epoch in my life…No man ever was in Love with a woman of forty, since the Deluge. A Boy may be so, but that blaze of straw only lasts till he is old enough to distinguish between Youth and Age.'

Algarotti returns to the apparently more fascinating charms of the Prussian Court and Lady Mary, now aged

53, travels to Genoa, Geneva and into France. She will
never see her husband, Edward, again although they cor-
respond regularly on practical and family matters.

To Venice

Crossing the downs to Dover,
roadside flowers
white with chalk dust –
clouds of when I was five,
my grandmother's house.

*

At Calais they took
a pound of my snuff;
left me the jewels –
duty free.

*

A good friend –
the only passport
to happiness.

*

I've crossed the Alps before.
I didn't like it then.
I don't like it now.
They are too big
for someone in a basket
who can't stop shivering.

*

Venus's floating city –
Love at first sight.

*

Blue sky and terracotta tiles,
shutters of cypress green,

ochre plaster, marble facades,
whirligig moorings capped with gold,

black and silver gondolas
ploughing oil-dark waters –

the whole city's a painting.

*

If I were a pyramid
on holiday, I couldn't
have had more visitors.

*

The fashion here's
for sixpenny masks
no one hides behind.

You do what you like.
No gossip or sneers.
Lace-trimmed liberty.

*

Christmas Day –
the sun shines
clear as midsummer.

*

Sometimes I can dream
myself back in Constantinople,
all those cupolas and campaniles,
the sound of slippers on stone.

*

My Lord Hervey, the charmer, says I paint
a picture of Venice in my letters
better than any by Canaletto.

*

Although you think you hold all the aces,
someone else is dealing the cards.
And, however you play, they're marked.

*

The tourists only speak English.
They come here to shop, to buy
new clothes they wear in cafes
where they meet just each other.
Once they've fallen in love
with a lady who waits on a diva,
they go back home, men of the world.

*

Ovid's ghost, this city and destiny
have turned me into a girl again,
all dressed up and dancing with princes,
kicking my heels in palaces.

If only a change of heart were as easy.

*

It's May and we're still sitting by firesides.
The sun has shrivelled into an old man
who's forgotten how to stare at the ladies.
I miss the blaze in the old rogue's eye.

*

Ascension Day – Mary rises
to her home in heaven
and the Doge marries the Sea.
A wedding of woman
and water – *il mare, la mer.*

*

At the Regatta –
seahorses and stars
on the water,
doves and roses,
gardens in gondolas
with silver oars.

*

Walking through the narrow alleys,
under the arches, over the bridges,
just when I think I've caught her,
the right words in the right places,
I see there are only threads
in my hand,
        a few feathers,
                a smudge of scarlet.

*

Of course I fell in love with her –
La Serenissima. There is no other.
It's like looking in a mirror
and just staying there, never turning away.

*

I want better ink.

*

This place is infested with English,
a plague of frogs and lice
in my Pharaoh's palace.
Time to fly south.

When in Rome

Every night I walk in a new garden
and every night I'm sad as Tantalus.
Living with beauty is unbearable
as not living with beauty. This fresh ache
I locate somewhere in the old country,
the lost landscape of my heart, is snakebite,
is acres of yellow sand. Only time
will cure it, that merciless doctor.

The trees are dancers; they sway together
and alone. I bathe in the blessing
of their blue-gold evening light. I so want
to be wrong about love, this cruel yearning.
Anything but the raw thorns of silence,
the tangle of too many thoughts, the burr.

Let the fountains be full of forgetting.
I will eat no more poisoned apples.
May I find my paradise, where I might
call myself contented, my heartland.

Apocryphal

The Captain warned me of red sky, of storms
to the North. I wrapped my courage around me
like a big-buckled belt but stayed all day
below deck, in the smallest room, reading

poems about shipwrecks, between sips of rum.
Lost enough on land, why should I fear
water? I could hear the wind keening,
rattling the rigging like dead men's bones.

I scribbled a couplet on the wall,
some borrowed lines, a reminder of one
who was sailing after her gale-blown dreams,
unfathomable, uncharted seas.

At Genoa I paid the kind Captain
with the treasure of an emerald ring,
meant to protect the wearer's chastity.
I didn't think I'd need it any more:

my forged love, a bauble of coloured glass.

Appetite for Love
(for F.A. again)

I was so hungry
my belly echoed
with emptiness.
I fell for him
like a starving man
set free
in a King's kitchen.
At last I said 'yes',
after thin years
of shaking my head.
I surrendered
to my greed
and gorged myself
on his tasty flesh,
devoured him
by the dishful,
swallowed his sweetness.
A whole cellar
of the finest wine,
I drank it all,
my mouth open,
my bruised lips.
No wonder
I was sick.
No wonder he gave
me belly ache.

The Treaty of Turin
(for F.A. finally)

While Europe was preparing itself for war,
we became enemies who once were allies.

I'd waited two years and crossed a continent
to see him again, hoping we'd join forces

and flourish. But we disagreed on terms;
our ideas on government at odds.

We argued about power, in a state.
Used to autonomy, we couldn't give

anything away; we wouldn't surrender
ourselves. I told lies about policy,

withheld information. My plans fell apart.
For two years I was a small colony

in his Wholly Bogus Empire. This May
morning I leapt off the map, the end

of history, seeking asylum
in its unmarked grave, one of the wounded.

CHAPTER THE EIGHTH

In which Lady Mary settles in Avignon, writing home 'I endeavour to amuse myself here with all sorts of monastic employments, the conversation not being at all agreeable to me, and friendship in France as impossible to be attained as orange trees on the mountains of Scotland.'
When England formally declares war on France in 1744, her son joins the army fighting against the French and Spanish. He is a hero at the Battle of Fontenoy, promoted, then captured by the enemy.

Lady Mary hears news of the deaths of her friends Lord Hervey and Robert Walpole. She travels unaccompanied through Provence and Languedoc but on meeting the Count Palazzi, she gratefully accepts his offer to escort her through the war zone to Genoa and Brescia.

At home her cousin Henry Fielding publishes *Joseph Andrews* and Hogarth completes *Marriage à la Mode*.

The Colour Green

The last letter you sent before you died,
Hervey, made me laugh and cry like a child,
Every line a kind and cruel farewell.

Consult my own desires was your advice.
Open my eyes to contentment, pleasure.
Love would grow new leaves on trees black and dry.
Only you believed I could be as wise,
Undeluded, enlightened as Solomon,
Remember the taste of Paradise.

Grief and my star's caprice drown me in doubt.
Rage is a cold tide, foaming, white. I count
Every hour of the twenty years we shared,
Every day of what's left of my life – neither
Necessary – *your words* – nor enough.

Moon

I am a huntress, chasing the sun
across the sky and never netting it.
In the Temple of Diana my breath

is all I catch, watching the moon,
waiting for the war to end. I tell her
secrets about love I can't keep and

stalk a slither of her quiet shining.
I want to wrap myself in the scent
of her cool whiteness, that knack

she has for catching and letting go.

The Great Palazzi

The Count appeared suddenly like a magician
and, in a flurry of horses and sequins,
he tossed a veil over the war
and granted my wish for freedom.

He wove me like a ghost across the water
and, with a wave of his white-gloved hand,
let me be Venetian and then Spanish,
conjured rooms and coaches out of thin air.

His best trick was turning me back
into myself for the Austrian soldiers
to escort us north through cannon fire
and citadel while I didn't blink an eye.

Even magicians have mothers. He took me
home to his, a jewel cut and polished
by his absence, his risks. I watched
his fist grow wings, open into a dove.

CHAPTER THE NINTH

In which Lady Mary takes up residence in Gottolengo, near
Brescia. At some cost Palazzi assists.

Back in England her son enjoys a brief spell of respect-
ability, under the influence of Lord Sandwich: he is elected
MP for Huntingdon and later Secretary of the Peace Congress
of Aix-la-Chapelle. On her daughter's side of the family,
her son-in-law Bute is appointed Lord of the Bedchamber
to Frederick Prince of Wales.

In Lady Mary's absence, Horace Walpole publishes the
Town Eclogues again. Richardson's *Clarissa*, Fielding's
Tom Jones, Cleland's *Fanny Hill: Memoirs of a Woman of
Pleasure* and Gray's *Elegy Written in a Country Churchyard*
are all welcomed by a hungry and growing reading public.
Lady Mary is sent copies of all the bestsellers by her daugh-
ter, Lady Bute. Dr Johnson's *Dictionary of the English
Language* starts more arguments than it resolves and sets
the standard for originality, wit and opinionated thinking.
The flowering of knowledge and culture, confidence and
pride is reflected in the founding of the British Museum.

In England and her colonies in September 1752 everyone
loses 11 days when the New Style Gregorian Calendar is
adopted. It is deemed the only way to bring England, still
following the old Julian calendar, in line with the rest of
continental Europe. The Gregorian calendar had been
ratified in 1582 by Pope Gregory XIII as the most accurate
method of charting the solar year. The 26 second discrep-
ancy each year adds up to 1 day's difference every 3,323
years; unlike the Julian lag of 11½ minutes a year.

Lady Mary's son makes a bigamous marriage and is
briefly imprisoned in Paris for gambling and robbery. Lady
Mary becomes seriously ill again, probably with malaria.
It emerges that Palazzi has been swindling her but she is
philosophical: '...so many inevitable accidents thwart our
designs and limit our best laid projects, the poor efforts of
our utmost prudence and political schemes appear (I fancy)
in the eyes of some superior beings like the pecking of a
young linnet to break a wire cage, or the climbing of a
squirrel in a hoop. The moral needs no explanation. Let

us sing as cheerfully as we can in our impenetrable confine-
ment and crack our nuts with pleasure from the little store
that is allow'd us.'

After several unsuccessful attempts, she finally manages
to escape her confinement to make her home further south,
dividing her time between Venice and Padua.

Mirror

Without mirrors I could pretend.
I could choose to be beautiful.
Or invisible. I could be seed or bloom,
not old fruit past its best.
I could dream none of that mattered.

Aren't mirrors stories you tell yourself
when the truth isn't enough?
When you're living on the outside?
Is an absence of mirrors just
the story's shadow, the glass
turned to the wall after a death?

My face was tired of looking back
at itself and all the other faces looking
and looking. I wanted my mirror
to be Italy – *where* not *who* –
a framed view of hills and trees
and sunlight. A golden country.
No more quicksilver masks.

Fool's Gold

Show me a woman nearing sixty
keeping a man half her age
in horses and I will show you
a fool and her gold.

I count out coin, note and jewel,
hand over my own ransom.
What I don't give he takes
anyway. All that glitters.

He won't let me go. He swears
I'm his bright badge of honour,
wearing me down with his tears.
Those dark eyes, my fool's gold.

Gritting My Teeth

A sword piercing my cheek,
soft crease where I smile,
argent and rose; the twist
of silver, taste of metal, petals
opening and opening; my mouth
airless, slug full of tongue;
jaw sore as falling and my face
fat and slow. Nowhere
to go. I am all mouth
and no word is enough.

The surgeon's iron brands,
Satan's eyes glowing. I close
my own. Black-out burn
on my gums, a seared smell
and white dreamless sleep.
Acid on raw skin, medicine
of fire. Until my lips inch
themselves around air again,
say *thank you,* all those
other dangerous words.

The Art of Living

Chance brought me here but Choice made me stay.
Choosing to listen to what the Count had to say.

And soon I grew to love it. The air
suited me. The valley held me in its gaze.

The Count brought me the only chair
in the village with arms. I locked my doors

and put glass in all the windows, hung
tapestries to warm the cold stone walls.

His castle became my convent. I was
abbess and novice, my only visitors

the priests of the parish and we'd play
whist, a penny a corner, and argue

about religion. I'd rise with the sun
and work in my garden among the vines,

the fruit trees, my roses and jasmines.
I was famous for my salad, home-grown tea.

I kept birds and bees, silkworms and peacocks
and forgot about banter and fancy clothes.

I'd visit the Lake to take its steel waters,
charmed by its music, violins and lutes,

the lapping of its waves. So many things
I used to think were important I left behind,

living each day as if it might be my last,
as if I were the Queen of the Castle.

Rhetorical

Which is easiest: to catch the red ball
of the sun as it's falling in the west;
to chase after a flock of sparrows
and lay salt on their tails or to seek out
happiness, find it and keep it forever?

After Another Visit from the Doctor

Mending old lace –
patched in one place,
it comes away in another.

The Wisdom Tree

When I was a sapling, the same passions
that left me in tears swept away
most of the seeds of my wisdom tree
and watered what were left behind.

The one tree rooted in good soil grew
slowly, needing bucketsful of care
and luck with the weather. Now the leaves
of my life are ready to fall, it thrives.

Picaresque

The last pages of *this* volume
unfolding the story of my life
was an adventure to make you tremble
on the edge of your seat, a tragedy
to make you weep. Smollett or Fielding
couldn't have spun a more colourful tale.

I wrote it myself later – *triste,*
tristiore, tristissimo – how three times
in three years I tried to go south. Escape.
Always some ruse – my carriages broken,
my horses lamed, my maid taken ill,
bandits at large, rivers in flood.

The only bandit I needed to fear
was the one down the hall whispering
about *my protection*, how much it cost.
It was autumn when I finally left,
a good season for endings. We set off,
my four servants and myself, his armed guard.

At Fianello I was robbed for the last time.
For my own safety I feigned forgiveness.
But I wouldn't sign my name to his lies.
I'd had enough and he'd had plenty.
The dénouement of *his* plot was prison;
mine was Padua, Venice, another new beginning.

CHAPTER THE TENTH

In which Lady Mary establishes two homes in Venice and
in Padua and moves between the two. At the age of 68, she
revives her friendship and flirtation with Algarotti, the 'swan
of Padua'. The British Consul in Venice, Joseph Smith,
and his circle insult and harass her. This is to some extent
relieved by her growing attachment to Sir James Stuart and
his family. 'As I approach a second childhood, I endeavour
to enter in the pleasures of it.' She corresponds regularly
with her daughter on family matters and in particular the
upbringing and education of her grand-daughters. On the
death of her husband she decides to return to England.

At home, Hume publishes his *Enquiry Concerning
Human Understanding*, George II dies and is succeeded
by George III. His favourite, Bute, Lady Mary's son-in-
law, becomes Prime Minister.

Venice & Padua: Views

Palazzo Mocenigo

Mocenigo welcomes me back,
one of his city's prodigal daughters.
But nothing stays the same.
Not even Venice.

I shuttle across the lagoon
back and forth to Padua,
listening to all the clocks
in Europe ticking.

Piazza San Marco

Even the pigeons seem languid,
sad at what's passed
and what's still to come.

Palazzo Barbarigo

At the piano, a daughter
singing like a nightingale.

In the chair next to me, a man
whispering in London he'd heard
my daughter singing.

In the lobby outside, me
crying, like a lost mother.

The Bridge of Sighs

If this is the city of love,
it's also the city of death.
Listen: it's hard to tell why
someone is sighing in the dark.
Is it love or are they dying?

Who's to judge what are the deeds
of men and what's the work
of witches? I'm waiting to hear
stories of Lady Mary flying
on her broomstick, how she cast
spells on cows, bewitched a girl
to swallow pins and conjured
a toad from a man's groin.

I ask you, what do men fear most?
Women. Who do men scorn most?
The old. What is the worst monster
in all the world? *An old woman.*
Damned if she's a witch,
damned if she isn't.

The Grand Canal
TO MR WORTLEY MONTAGU

You write that it is only my letters
from abroad that go astray, suggesting
it's my fault. Or I do it on purpose.

These days my head is fat with fog
like the grey shadows that snaked over
the slow *s* of the canal all autumn.

I've come to believe we're no better
than straw floating on the water. The current
sweeps us along and we think we're swimming.

Now it's January it's warm as England
in May. I'm sending you something to warm
your feet, keep you at ease, hot as posset.

Palazzo Mangili Valmarana

The consul and his friends take great pleasure
in insulting, taunting and snubbing me.
I am enemy, scapegoat, laughing stock,
ignorant of my crime. They won't send me
the newspapers. They're turning
all the English against me. These are men
who think they're refined, think they're collectors.
They cultivate Vice and call it Art.

No more. I'm holding the card in my hand
over a candle flame to blacken it.
Ace of Spades. I etch some lines blotted
with rage and condemnation, toss it down
on the table and rise like a stiff wind,
leaving the double doors yawning, silence
behind me. It's cold out on the canal
but I'm hot and crazed. No shame.

My spirits in company are false fire.
I have a cool dampness inside me.
No wonder when three freedoms are denied
those of us condemned to petticoats –
Love, Vengeance and Poetry. What is a life
lived in silence? Whatever card we hold
in our hand, we will never win the game,
never conquer the chequered knavish kings.

In Padua

Like Voltaire's Candide what I do best,
what I love best is tending my garden.
My eyes are older than I am, worn out
with books, pen and paper. I can tell
green from green by the smell – rosemary,
basil, oregano, thyme – rub the leaves
between my fingers, let my nose name it,
the scent rising, beautiful in the air.

Small Pleasures

If I can't have love,
if I can't have vengeance
and if I can't travel
to Tübingen to see my friends,

I'm going to console myself
with an enormous bowlful
of the best oysters in Venice.

To the Imitator of Horace
(Mr Alexander Pope)

V

The art of satire is to slice brightly
through its victim's heart but your knife was blunt.
A clumsy hand. Too angry – a sure sign
of bad breeding, my dear. You couldn't make
up your mind if I was a chicken or
the wife of a farmer or a miser,
a whore with a silver tongue or plain filth.
What was plain: I was just what you feared most –
that dang'rous thing, a female wit. If that's
what a writer should do – take on his own
worst enemies, I admit, you did it.
In print. In couplets of scurrilous shit.

One of the needles in your little fist
was, the price of my fame, to twist a name
I admired into one to fit a jade,
stitch a dirty old petticoat of shame.
So I became *Sappho*, impossible,
unnatural, a female sun. That other
thing you feared: the secret love between two
friends. You stamped your foot like a child to prove
your manliness. Yes? I can't pretend none
of it hurt. These days I take some comfort
in keeping your work inside my closet
and wreak my revenge by shitting on it.

Trash, Lumber etc.

I know these will be some of my last days
but it feels more like I'm a child again.
Happy playing magpie, I buy bright baubles,
trinkets, new furnishings, arrange each piece
around me, a private world of pleasure.

Inside the cocoon of it, I read,
stacking my days, nights too, with pillars of books.
Anything will do as long as there are words,
the chase and soothe of someone else's story.
No doubt they're all so much trash and lumber.

Age has taught me valuable books
are as rare as valuable men.
I must be content with what I can find,
ignore the too-loud whispers – *Old Lady
Mary, trash and lumber* – my failing eyes.

Algarotti's Cleopatra

In Padua, once all the jackals of Lust
and Money were poisoned and their sisters,
Illusion and Fame, run through with swords,
at last we could sigh, my swan and I,
and sit across a table as friends.

I heard he told Tiepolo to touch up
his Cleopatra, tint her blonde to brunette.
Someone whispered she was the image of me
when I was young and stunning, when the dash
I cut made men quake. A fitting tribute
to one who once lost, in less than a fortnight,
her homeland as well as her heart.
The strongest women fall the hardest.

As if we'd only paused mid-sentence,
fifteen years later we carried on talking.
For old times' sake, we still flirted.
And I always wore my golden bracelets.

A Wreath of Feathers

(on the death of Edward Wortley Montagu)

Over half a century we spanned
together, a bridge engineered by
our own good wishes, defying
time and distance. The day it broke
I was left hanging in mid-air, holding
my breath, waiting for earth to rise up
and meet me, fold me under its black wings.
I fell into a room glittering
with mirrors, all scrawled with jackdaw ink.
My mouth wrote a thin line, full of nothing,
and nowhere, nameless, was the best place.
A dead end to the road. I felt the wind
whistle through my bones and let it blow
them back upstream. That river called home.

CHAPTER THE ELEVENTH

In which Lady Mary travels home to England. Stopping in
the port of Rotterdam to recoup, she entrusts the *Embassy
Letters* to one Reverend Benjamin Sowden. She is welcomed
back to London like a diva, an almost mythical survivor.
Meanwhile in Venice her son, unregenerate, forges her sig-
nature to obtain money.

Lady Mary writes her last letter in July to Lady Frances
Stuart: 'Dear Madam, – I have been ill a long time, and am
now so bad I am little capable of writing, but I would not
pass in your opinion as either stupid or ungrateful. My heart
is always warm in your service, and I am always told your
affairs shall be taken care of. You may depend, dear madam,
nothing will be wanting on the part of – your ladyship's
faithful humble servant...'

Not in good health when she left Venice, Lady Mary
dies of breast cancer on 21st August, just as Rousseau's
Social Contract is published in France and Sarah Scott's
Millennium Hall appears in England. The following year
the *Embassy Letters* are published, having been stolen from
Sowden for a night and copied before he was able to sub-
mit them to Lady Mary's daughter, who destroyed many
of her diaries and writings.

Lady Mary Lazarus

I'd done it so many times before
it was easy. And even dead women
tell tales. Who do you think
you're listening to now?
Look at your face in the mirror.
Find the signs of pox, skin's slow decay.
Death. Remember, whatever else happens,
you'll do it too. Isn't it worth
a few rehearsals to get it right?

She wants to get it right
so she comes back from the dead,
from the city of life and death
and love, is it, brings her back?
My daughter. My house is a cupboard,
a kennel, a harpsichord.
Too many people are talking at once.
You know what it's like when
too many people are talking at once.

The only thing to do is keep talking
yourself and while you're talking
you know you're alive. You can tell
because I'm dressed in yellow velvet
and sables and someone is saying
I have beautiful eyes. She still
has very beautiful eyes. She's still more
alive than fifteen people together
and she'll never, I'll never, you'll never forget her.

Heliotrope

Under my left breast, my heart.
A woman's wounds, her blood.
A seed takes root like a secret
and blooms into a beautiful
ulcerous scarlet flower.
An English rose. Home.

Hemlock has a purple taste. Opium
is crimson, fading to pink.
Raw meat. All there is left of me.
While the rest of me is strong
and cooked. Eat me, sky,
swallow me. A new, blue country.

Sic Transit Gloria Mundi

I leave

to my daughter
  everything I own

to my son
  one guinea

to the Duchess of Portland
  the ring I bought with her mother's legacy –
  a white diamond

to Chiara Michiel
  her choice of all my other rings

to James Stuart Mackenzie
  my large gold octagon snuff box

to Dr Mora
  five hundred pounds

to each of my servants
  a year's wages (eight pounds for the men,
  four pounds for the women) and for the foreigners
  their expenses to take them home

to my maid, Mari Anna
  a year's wages (twenty-five pounds),
  travelling expenses home
  plus ten guineas more
  and all my clothes and linen

to Joshua Reynolds, painter
  a butterfly ring, wings studded with diamonds and rubies,
  body of emeralds, hoop chased with poppy leaves,
  buds and flowers set with amethysts, diamonds, topaz and quartz
  and engraved *Sic Transit Gloria Mundi*

NOTES

The Toast of the Kit-Cat Club
This happened when Lady Mary was eight. She was the only female ever to be admitted to the fashionable Whig club.

'The first year I was married'
Sometime during 1712-13 Lady Mary wrote the poem 'Written ex tempore in Company in a Glass Window the first year I was marry'd'. It was printed (inaccurately) as 'The Lady's Resolve' in the *Plain Dealer* in 1724 and much reprinted.

First Fruit
Pineapples were still very rare and much prized. It was several years later that the first pineapple was cultivated in England (by Sir Matthew Decker at his house in Richmond).

Border Country
Wortley Montagu's ambassadorial mission was to work towards a peace treaty between Austria and Turkey. There had been a long-standing struggle for power between the Austro-Hungarian and the Ottoman Empires. As it turned out he failed as he was considered too conciliatory towards the Turks and was recalled in 1718. Crossing the Battlefield of Peterwardein, Lady Mary witnessed nearly 30,000 corpses, still unburied, scattered in the snow.

Adrianople, April
From Lady Mary's letters: 'They repeated over and over to me; *Üzelle, pek üzelle*, which is nothing but *charming, very charming*.'

'When the pashas travel 'tis yet worse. Those oppressors are not content with eating all that is to be eaten belonging to the peasants; after they have crammed themselves and their numerous retinue they have the impudence to exact what they call teeth money, a contribution for the use of their teeth, worn with doing them the honour of devouring their meat.'
(This in villages in the land between Belgrade and Adrianople.)

'Here are some birds held in a sort of religious reverence and for that reason, multiply prodigiously: turtles [doves] on account of their innocence and storks because they are supposed to make every winter the pilgrimage to Mecca. To say truth they are the happiest subjects under the Turkish government, and are so sensible of their privileges they walk the streets without fear and generally build in the low parts of houses. Happy are those who are so distinguished. The vulgar Turks are perfectly persuaded that they will not be that year attacked either by fire or pestilence. I have the happiness of one of their sacred nests under my chamber window.'

'their shapes are also wholly concealed by a thing they call a "ferace" which no woman of any sort appears without. This has straight sleeves that reaches to their finger ends and it laps all round them, not unlike a riding hood. In winter it is of cloth and in summer plain stuff or silk. You may guess then how effectually this disguises them, that there is no distinguishing the great lady from her slave and 'tis impossible for the most jealous husband to know his wife when he meets her, and no man dare either touch or follow a woman in the street.'

kalpak: a cap 'in winter of fine velvet embroidered with pearls or diamonds and in summer of a light shining silver stuff. This is fixed on one side of the head, hanging a little way down with a gold tassel, and bound on either with a circle of diamonds (as I have seen several) or a rich embroidered handkerchief'.

Recipe to Prevent the Smallpox
In Turkey Lady Mary chose to follow the local custom and have her son in-oculated against smallpox. Back in England she inoculated her daughter and convinced others, including the Princess of Wales, to do the same with their own children. Although initially reluctant, British doctors adopted the pro-cedure. Lady Mary criticised them for their departures from her advice, cutting into the skin too deeply and inserting too large a quantity of the live virus. In return she was pilloried as an amateur and quack, whose priority was simply the preservation of beauty rather than of life itself. It was not until the work of Edward Jenner nearly 80 years later that the medical profession accepted the effectiveness of the practice of vaccination based on the same principle.

To the Imitator of Horace
In 1733 Lady Mary collaborated with Lord Hervey on 'Verses Address'd to the Imitator of the First Satire of the Second Book of Horace' in response to Pope's 'Imitation', published earlier that year. As well as other insults aimed at Lord Hervey, this couplet was directed at Lady Mary:
> From furious Sappho scarce a milder Fate
> P-x'd by her love, or libell'd by her Hate.

Earlier Pope, corresponding with Lady Mary during her travels in Turkey, had written: 'If ever you come again, I shall never be able to behave with decency …Come for God's sake, come Lady Mary, come quickly!'

III: In 1722 Pope met Judith Cowper (later Madan), a younger, more compli-ant object for his admiration, to whom he addressed poems and compliments, using the same images and phrases he had already showered on Lady Mary.

IV:
> What dire offence from amorous causes springs,
> What mighty contests rise from trivial things…

The opening lines of Pope's 'The Rape of the Lock' (1712/14).

Moon
In Avignon Lady Mary lived in her very own Temple of Diana: 'I try to content myself with reading, working, walking, and what you'll wonder to hear me mention, building. I know not whether you saw when you were at Avignon the rock of Douse, at the foot of which is the vice-legate's palace; from the top of it you may see the four provinces of Venaisin, Provence, Languedoc, and Dauphine; with the distant mountains of Auvergne, and the near meeting

of the Durance and Rhône which flow under it; in short, it is the most beautiful land-prospect I ever saw. There was anciently a temple of Diana, and another of Hercules of Gaul, whose ruins were turned into a fort, where the powder and ammunition of the town were kept, which was destroyed by lightning, about eighty years since. There remained an ancient round tower, which I said in presence of the consul would make a very agreeable belvidere if it was mine. I expected no consequence from the accidental speech of mine; but he proposed to the Hôtel de Ville, the next day, making me a present of it…I have fitted up a little pavilion, which Lord Burlington would call a temple; being in the figure of the Rotunda; where I keep my books and generally pass all my evenings.'

The Great Palazzi
Palazzi is first referred to in the letters as 'a gentleman of the bedchamber of the prince (of Saxony), who is a man of the first quality in this province'.

Mirror
In 1746 after her illness, Lady Mary saw her reflection in a mirror and found it 'so disagreeable, I resolv'd to spare my selfe such mortifications for the Future'.

Gritting My Teeth
In 1750 an infection of Lady Mary's gums became gangrenous. The best surgeon in Cremona was summoned and 'immediately apply'd red hot Irons to [her] Gumms'. The barbaric treatment continued when several days later caustics were laid onto her seared gums. To everyone's surprise Lady Mary survived but she said it was the 'severest illness I ever had'. It took her several months to recover.

To the Imitator of Horace
v: Lady Mary celebrated her quarrels with Pope, Swift and Bolingbroke by having the bowl of her commode decorated with engravings of their books. She told Francis Hutchinson that she had 'the satisfaction of shitting on them every day'.